THE GRUESOME GUIDE TO WORLD MONSTERS

TO RUTH & LARRY STOTTER
J. S.

TO WING
H. D.

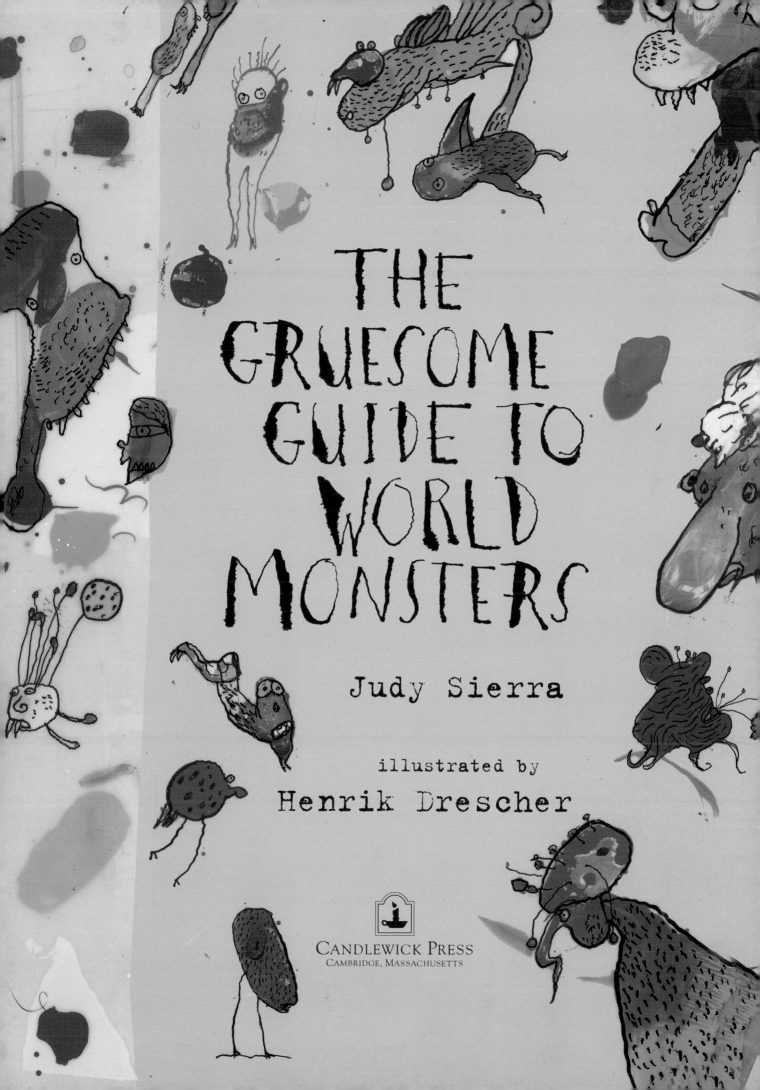

THE GRUESOME GUIDE TO WORLD MONSTERS

Judy Sierra

illustrated by

Henrik Drescher

CANDLEWICK PRESS
CAMBRIDGE, MASSACHUSETTS

When you plan a vacation, do you buy a travel guide?

There are many good books ☠ or overcoming *some* of these about restaurants, museums, monsters, *some* of the time. I have hotels, and interesting sights, but searched books and journals for until now there has never been a this information so that I could guide to the monsters that live pass it along to you. You will learn throughout the world. First the how each creature behaves and good news. From Alaska to where it lives. Of course, because Argentina, and from Nigeria to modern air and sea transportation New Zealand, the woods and are so efficient, a *mansusopsop,* a water holes are teeming with *nundu,* or a *kwanokasha* might bizarre and fascinating creatures already be living in your who are eager to meet tourists and neighborhood. travelers. The bad news is that few tourists and travelers ever live to tell about them.

This guide will help you plan how to meet—and more important, how to flee from—the world's most terrifying inhabitants. There are proven methods for escaping

A FINAL DISCLAIMER: I did not make any of this up. These monsters are a genuine part of the world's folklore and have lived in people's imaginations and dreams for thousands of years. See the afterword for more information about why people believe in these creatures.

GRUESOMENESS RATINGS

☠	☠☠	☠☠☠	☠☠☠☠	☠☠☠☠☠
FRIGHTENING This monster is scary but not life-threatening.	**DANGEROUS** Smart travelers can avoid or overcome this monster.	**VERY DANGEROUS** Your chances of surviving a meeting with this monster are 50-50 at best.	**USUALLY FATAL** Avoid this monster at all costs. Encounters are usually fatal.	**FATAL** Once this monster sees you, it's too late.

CONTENTS

NORTH AMERICA 6

CENTRAL AND SOUTH AMERICA 18

EUROPE 28

AFRICA 40

ASIA AND THE PACIFIC 50

AFTERWORD 64

BLOODY MARY

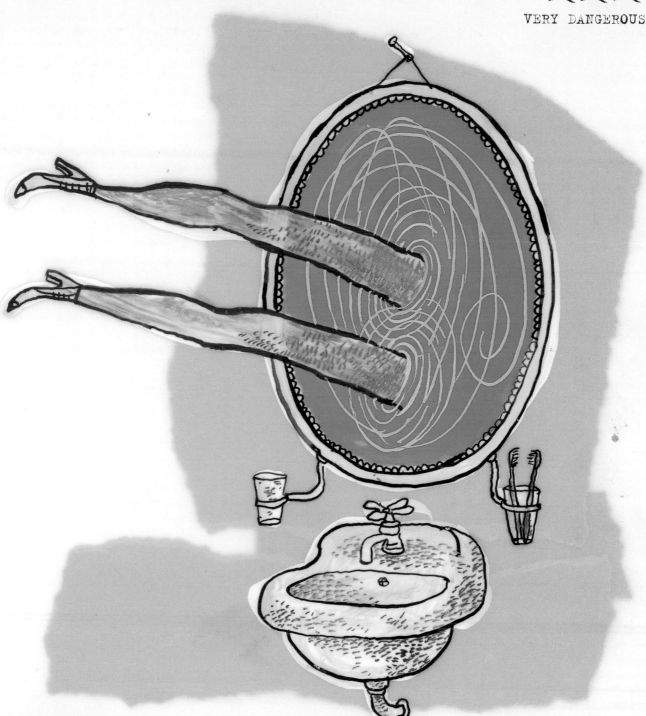

LOCATION: Entire continent

GRUESOMENESS RATING: 3

DESCRIPTION: Bloody Mary is an evil specter who lives on the other side of mirrors, especially the mirrors of elementary-school bathrooms. Bloody Mary will reach out and grab you, but only if you see her first. Foolish children who want to see Bloody Mary, light candles in a dark bathroom and repeat "Bloody Mary, Bloody Mary" until her face appears.

SURVIVAL TIP: No one has ever returned from the other side of the mirror, though some have managed to pull away at the last minute, with only the gashes and scratches of Bloody Mary's fingernails as souvenirs. For maximum safety, stay far away from mirrors, or better yet, don't look in them at all.

ALKUNTANE

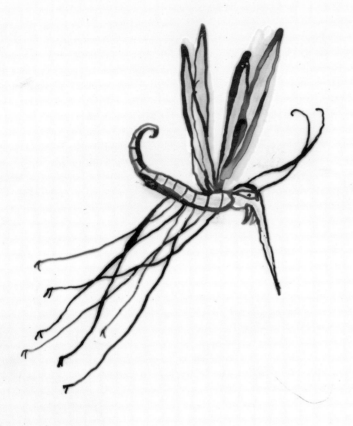

LOCATION: Pacific Northwest

GRUESOMENESS RATING: 3

DESCRIPTION: These tiny vampires look and sound like mosquitoes. Once they enter your ear, they are capable of drilling through your skull and sucking out your brains.

SURVIVAL TIP: Cover your ears at all times. If you see a dark bubble emerging from someone else's ear, it is probably an *alkuntane*. Yank it out and quickly cover your own ears.

WANAGEMESWAK

LOCATION: Northeastern United States

GRUESOMENESS RATING: 4

DESCRIPTION: These small, elusive creatures live in lakes and rivers. They are so thin that you can see them only from the side. Head-on, they are invisible. *Wanagemeswak* often attack and kill swimmers with their sharp, hatchet-like faces. They are fond of making little dolls from clay, which they leave beside the water to dry. If you find a *wanagemeswak* doll, it will bring you good luck.

SURVIVAL TIP: Swim only in the hotel pool.

8

SNEE-NEE-IQ

LOCATION: Pacific Northwest

GRUESOMENESS RATING: 2

DESCRIPTION: The *snee-nee-iq* is a tall, bony-legged creature who kidnaps children and carries them home in a basket. She sneaks around late at night, following the cries of bad children who won't go to bed. When the *snee-nee-iq* returns to her camp with her basket full of children, she smokes some of them over a fire, like salmon. Then she hangs them on tree branches until she is ready to eat them.

SURVIVAL TIP: Go to bed quietly and on time.

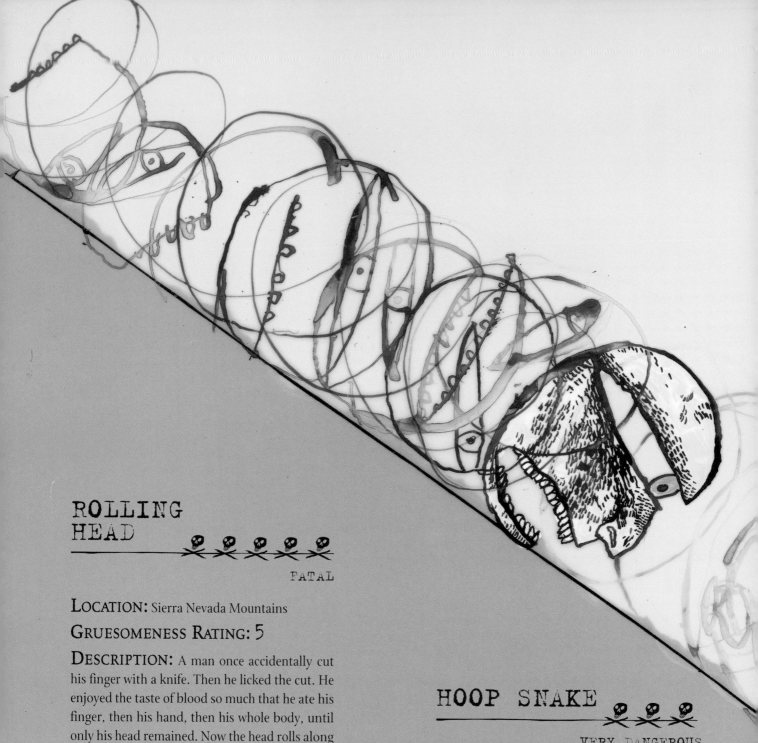

ROLLING HEAD

FATAL

LOCATION: Sierra Nevada Mountains

GRUESOMENESS RATING: 5

DESCRIPTION: A man once accidentally cut his finger with a knife. Then he licked the cut. He enjoyed the taste of blood so much that he ate his finger, then his hand, then his whole body, until only his head remained. Now the head rolls along the ground, biting and greedily devouring anyone in its path.

SURVIVAL TIP: Sorry, none available.

HOOP SNAKE

VERY DANGEROUS

LOCATION: Southwestern United States

GRUESOMENESS RATING: 3

DESCRIPTION: The hoop snake is an extremely long reptile that can grab the tip of its tail with its mouth and roll after its victims at high speed, faster than the fastest car. The bite of the hoop snake is fatal, as there is no known antidote for its venom.

SURVIVAL TIP: The only way to escape this snake is to jump right through its hoop as it rolls. This confuses the snake. It lets go of its tail and flops helplessly to the ground.

UKTENA

☠ ☠ ☠ ☠ ☠

FATAL

LOCATION: Southeastern United States

GRUESOMENESS RATING: 5

DESCRIPTION: The *uktena* is a long water serpent with horns on its head. It feeds on children and fishermen who get too close to its home. Brave and foolish people are always hunting the *uktena,* hoping to gain possession of the magic crystal inside its head that cures all diseases. The crystal is a dangerous treasure, though. It will keep its magic power only as long as its owner feeds it human blood every day.

SURVIVAL TIP: Don't go near rivers or lakes.

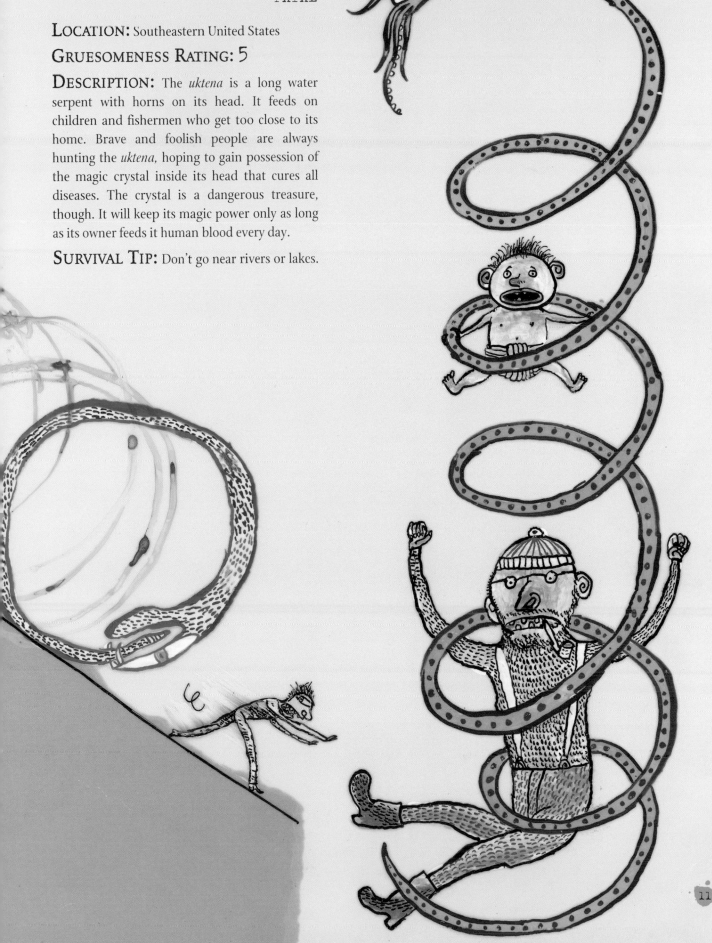

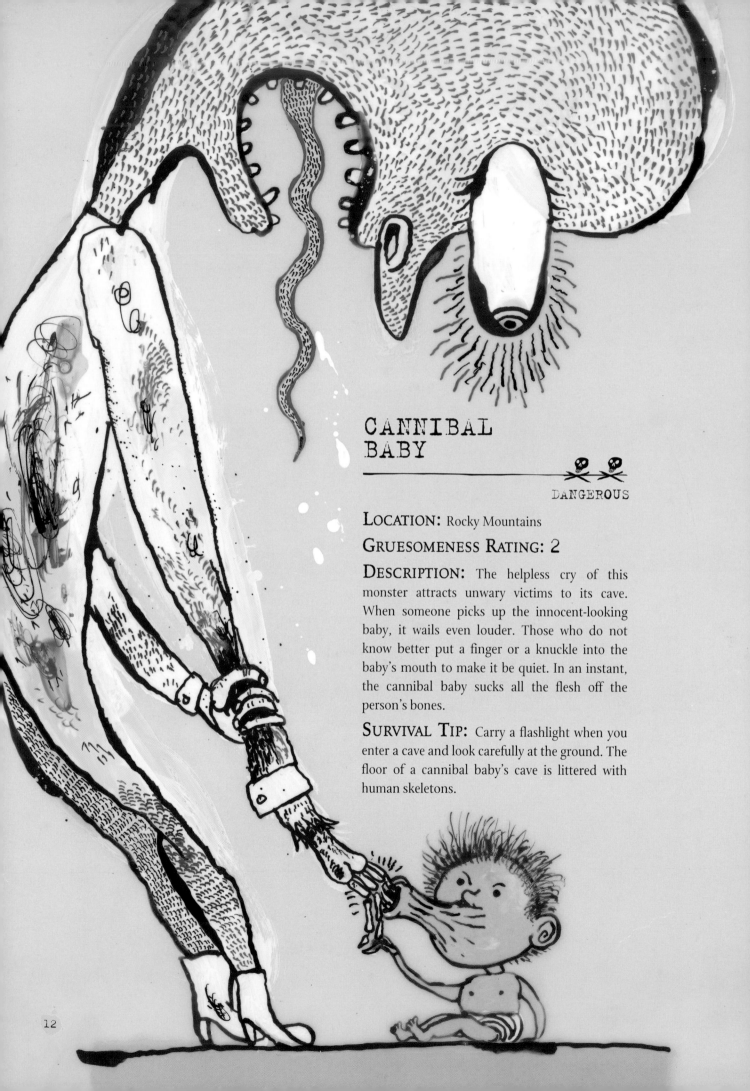

CANNIBAL BABY

DANGEROUS

LOCATION: Rocky Mountains

GRUESOMENESS RATING: 2

DESCRIPTION: The helpless cry of this monster attracts unwary victims to its cave. When someone picks up the innocent-looking baby, it wails even louder. Those who do not know better put a finger or a knuckle into the baby's mouth to make it be quiet. In an instant, the cannibal baby sucks all the flesh off the person's bones.

SURVIVAL TIP: Carry a flashlight when you enter a cave and look carefully at the ground. The floor of a cannibal baby's cave is littered with human skeletons.

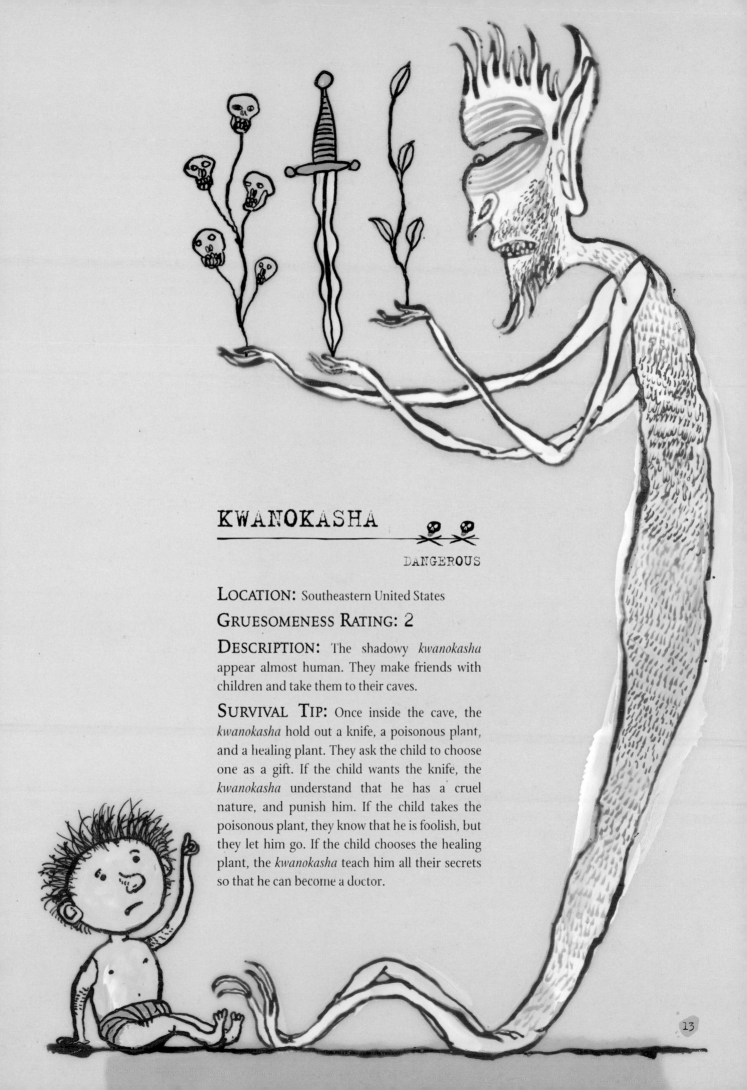

KWANOKASHA

DANGEROUS

LOCATION: Southeastern United States

GRUESOMENESS RATING: 2

DESCRIPTION: The shadowy *kwanokasha* appear almost human. They make friends with children and take them to their caves.

SURVIVAL TIP: Once inside the cave, the *kwanokasha* hold out a knife, a poisonous plant, and a healing plant. They ask the child to choose one as a gift. If the child wants the knife, the *kwanokasha* understand that he has a cruel nature, and punish him. If the child takes the poisonous plant, they know that he is foolish, but they let him go. If the child chooses the healing plant, the *kwanokasha* teach him all their secrets so that he can become a doctor.

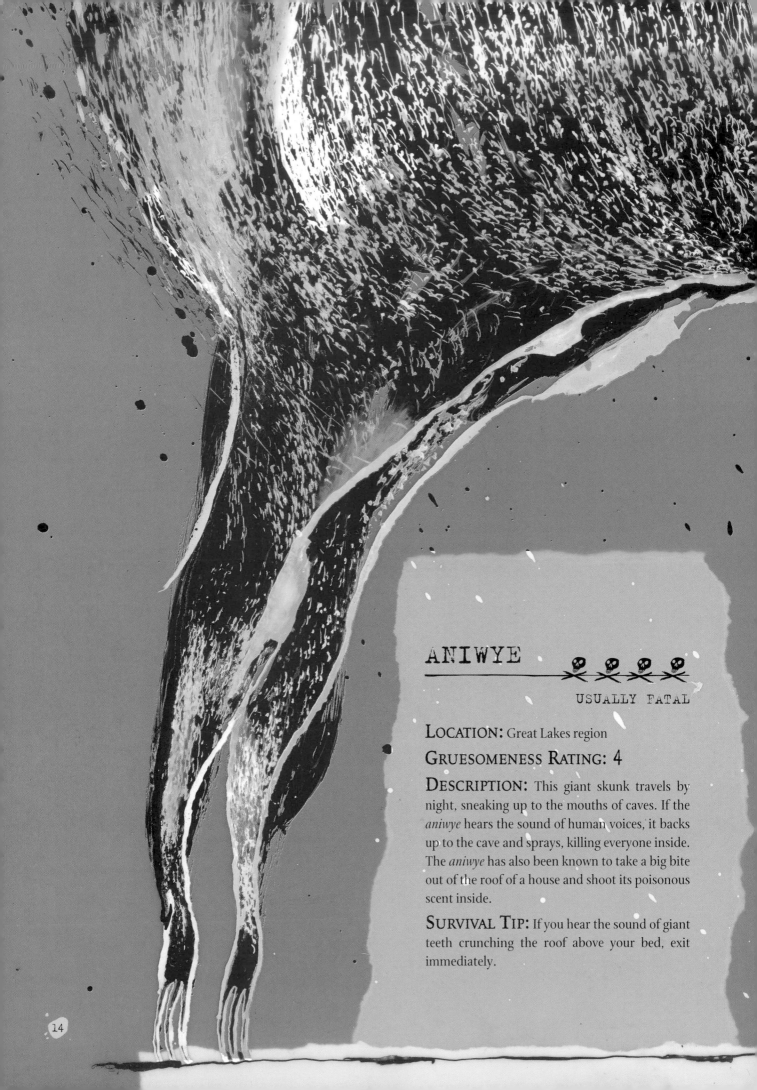

ANIWYE

USUALLY FATAL

LOCATION: Great Lakes region

GRUESOMENESS RATING: 4

DESCRIPTION: This giant skunk travels by night, sneaking up to the mouths of caves. If the *aniwye* hears the sound of human voices, it backs up to the cave and sprays, killing everyone inside. The *aniwye* has also been known to take a big bite out of the roof of a house and shoot its poisonous scent inside.

SURVIVAL TIP: If you hear the sound of giant teeth crunching the roof above your bed, exit immediately.

OCASTA 💀💀💀💀💀

FATAL

LOCATION: Southeastern United States

GRUESOMENESS RATING: 5

DESCRIPTION: No weapon can hurt the giant *ocasta* because his entire body is covered with slabs of flint. He carries a magic walking staff. When he throws the staff across a chasm, it creates a phantom bridge that disappears as soon as he walks over it. This staff also guides the *ocasta* to his favorite food, human livers.

SURVIVAL TIP: No survivors have been located.

WATER BABIES 💀💀

DANGEROUS

LOCATION: Great Plains

GRUESOMENESS RATING: 2

DESCRIPTION: Water babies are small creatures that live in lakes and rivers. They are no bigger than a one-year-old child, but they are not really babies. They cry like babies in order to attract humans to the water's edge. Then they pull them in and eat them.

SURVIVAL TIP: Water babies will never harm children who throw their baby teeth into a lake or a river.

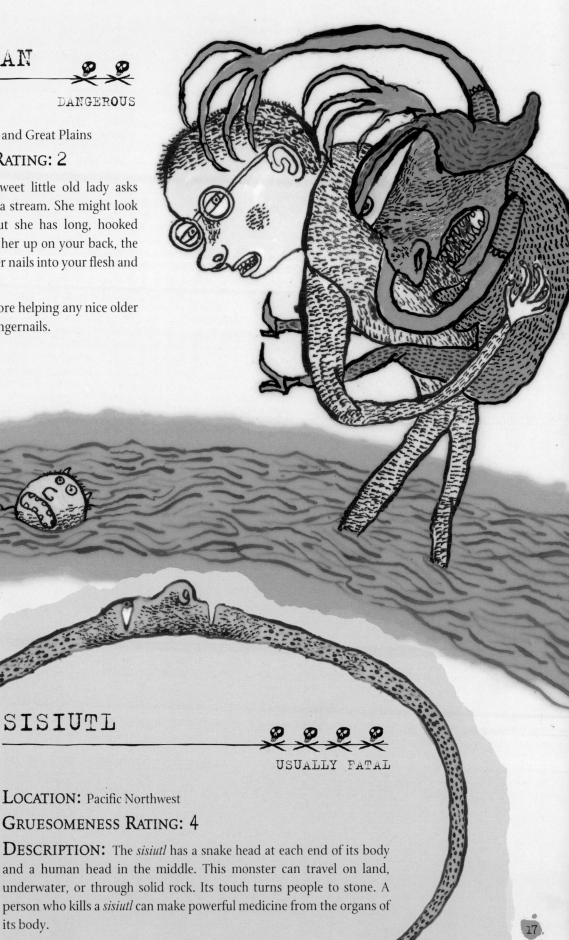

BURR WOMAN

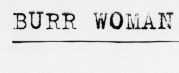

DANGEROUS

LOCATION: Midwest and Great Plains

GRUESOMENESS RATING: 2

DESCRIPTION: A sweet little old lady asks you to carry her across a stream. She might look like a grandmother, but she has long, hooked fingernails. If you hoist her up on your back, the burr woman will sink her nails into your flesh and never let go.

SURVIVAL TIP: Before helping any nice older ladies, ask to see their fingernails.

SISIUTL

USUALLY FATAL

LOCATION: Pacific Northwest

GRUESOMENESS RATING: 4

DESCRIPTION: The *sisiutl* has a snake head at each end of its body and a human head in the middle. This monster can travel on land, underwater, or through solid rock. Its touch turns people to stone. A person who kills a *sisiutl* can make powerful medicine from the organs of its body.

SURVIVAL TIP: Only a holly leaf can injure or kill a *sisiutl*.

17

Central and South America

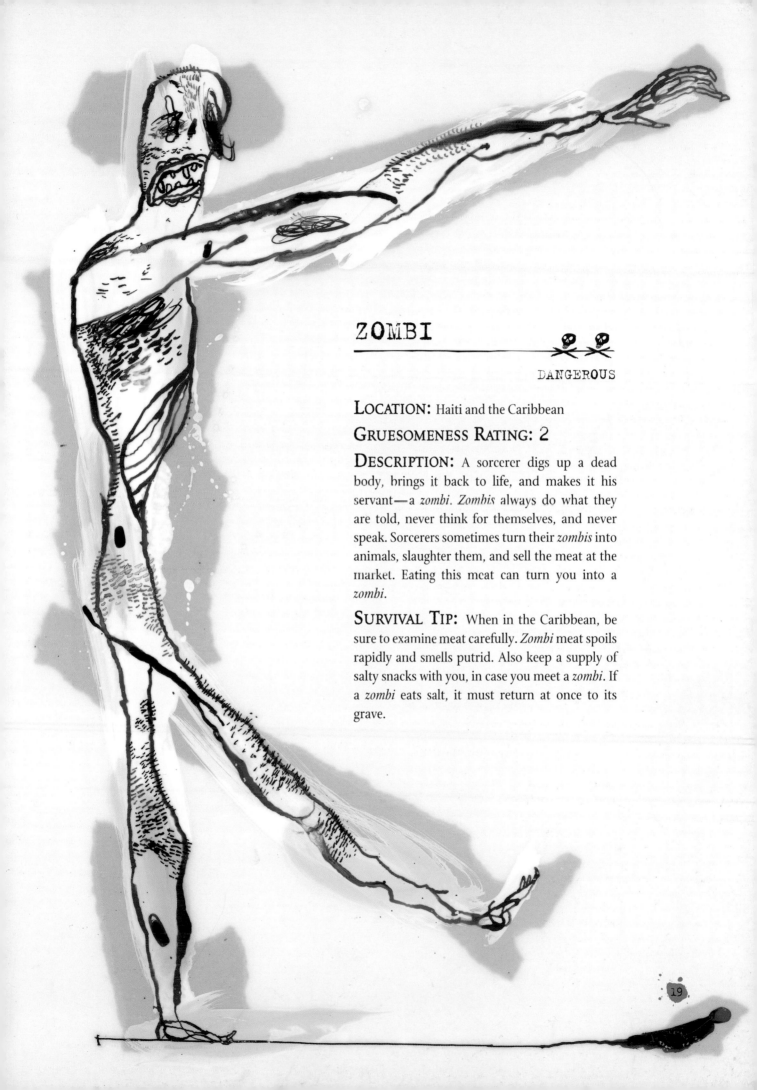

ZOMBI

LOCATION: Haiti and the Caribbean

GRUESOMENESS RATING: 2

DESCRIPTION: A sorcerer digs up a dead body, brings it back to life, and makes it his servant—a *zombi*. *Zombis* always do what they are told, never think for themselves, and never speak. Sorcerers sometimes turn their *zombis* into animals, slaughter them, and sell the meat at the market. Eating this meat can turn you into a *zombi*.

SURVIVAL TIP: When in the Caribbean, be sure to examine meat carefully. *Zombi* meat spoils rapidly and smells putrid. Also keep a supply of salty snacks with you, in case you meet a *zombi*. If a *zombi* eats salt, it must return at once to its grave.

CAPÉ-LOBO

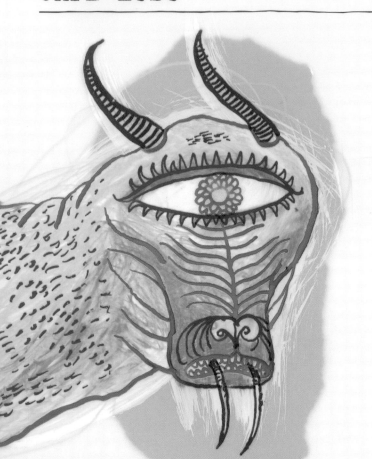

LOCATION: Brazil

GRUESOMENESS RATING: 2

DESCRIPTION: Deep in the Amazon rain forest lives the one-eyed *capé-lobo*. Its high-pitched cry can be heard ten miles away. The sound will often burst a hunter's eardrums. This creature feeds mainly on dogs and goats, but will also kill any person foolish enough to hunt on a Sunday. The *capé-lobo* has no feet, so its footprints are perfectly round. Bullets bounce off its hide.

SURVIVAL TIP: The *capé-lobo* can be killed only if a spear pierces its eye or bellybutton.

AZEMAN

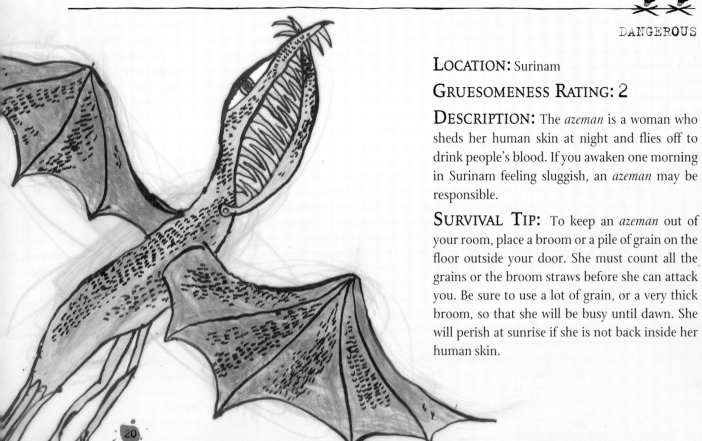

LOCATION: Surinam

GRUESOMENESS RATING: 2

DESCRIPTION: The *azeman* is a woman who sheds her human skin at night and flies off to drink people's blood. If you awaken one morning in Surinam feeling sluggish, an *azeman* may be responsible.

SURVIVAL TIP: To keep an *azeman* out of your room, place a broom or a pile of grain on the floor outside your door. She must count all the grains or the broom straws before she can attack you. Be sure to use a lot of grain, or a very thick broom, so that she will be busy until dawn. She will perish at sunrise if she is not back inside her human skin.

AKALAKUI

LOCATION: Venezuela

GRUESOMENESS RATING: 2

DESCRIPTION: The *akalakui* arc very small human-like creatures. They roam around in groups, calling *Vi, vi, vi!* They attack people who travel alone, shooting them with tiny poison arrows. Then they carry their victims back to their caves, crying *Shiwiwi, shiwiwi!* Those who escape the *akalakui* lose the ability to speak because the little guys tie their tongues in knots.

SURVIVAL TIP: One survivor of an *akalakui* attack learned how to cure himself in a dream. He locked himself in a hut for four days, then bathed in alcohol. Afterward he cooked a feast for everyone in his village, and could speak again.

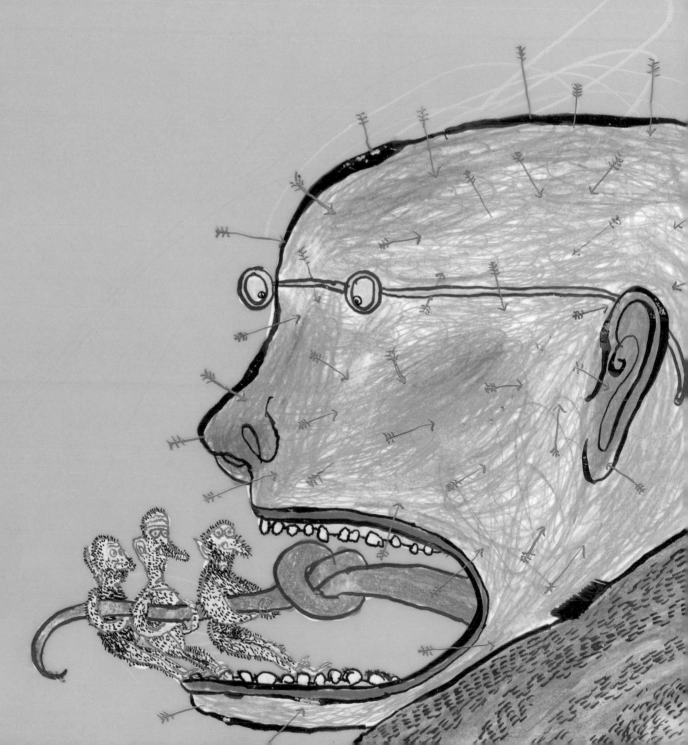

CURUPIRA

LOCATION: Brazil

GRUESOMENESS RATING: 2

DESCRIPTION: The *curupira* looks like any short, bald, blue man, except that he has only one eye in the middle of his forehead, a mouth full of shining, emerald green teeth, and feet that point backward. He is the guardian of the animals of the rain forest. If a hunter kills too many animals or kills simply for fun, the *curupira* will take revenge, sneaking up behind the hunter as he sleeps. He massages his victim's body until it is as soft as a ripe avocado, bites off his head, sucks out all his organs, then leaves the empty skin hanging on a tree branch as a warning to others who would kill more game than necessary.

SURVIVAL TIP: If you carelessly break the *curupira*'s hunting rules, offer him tobacco. He cannot resist it and will let you go.

LA COBRA GRANDE

FATAL

LOCATION: Brazil

GRUESOMENESS RATING: 5

DESCRIPTION: This snake-like monster lives in the rivers and lakes of the Amazon region, where it grows to be a thousand feet long. Traveling by night, the beast makes a deep rumbling noise, its eyes emitting beams like searchlights. It has the power to draw boats toward itself, like a magnet. Its gaze paralyzes people so that they stand perfectly still as they are devoured by *la cobra grande*.

SURVIVAL TIP: Sorry, no survivors to query.

CHONCHÓN

VERY DANGEROUS

LOCATION: Peru

GRUESOMENESS RATING: 3

DESCRIPTION: By day, a *chonchón* looks pretty much like an ordinary person. At night, he sends his head flying off to attack people and suck their blood, using his ears as wings.

SURVIVAL TIP: In Peru, stay far away from anyone with big floppy ears. He or she may become a *chonchón* after sunset. You can tell that a *chonchón* is nearby by its cry: *Tué, tué, tué!* The only way to ward off an attack is to say a particular chant or spread your jacket on the ground in a special way. Both are secret and known only to a few lucky Peruvians.

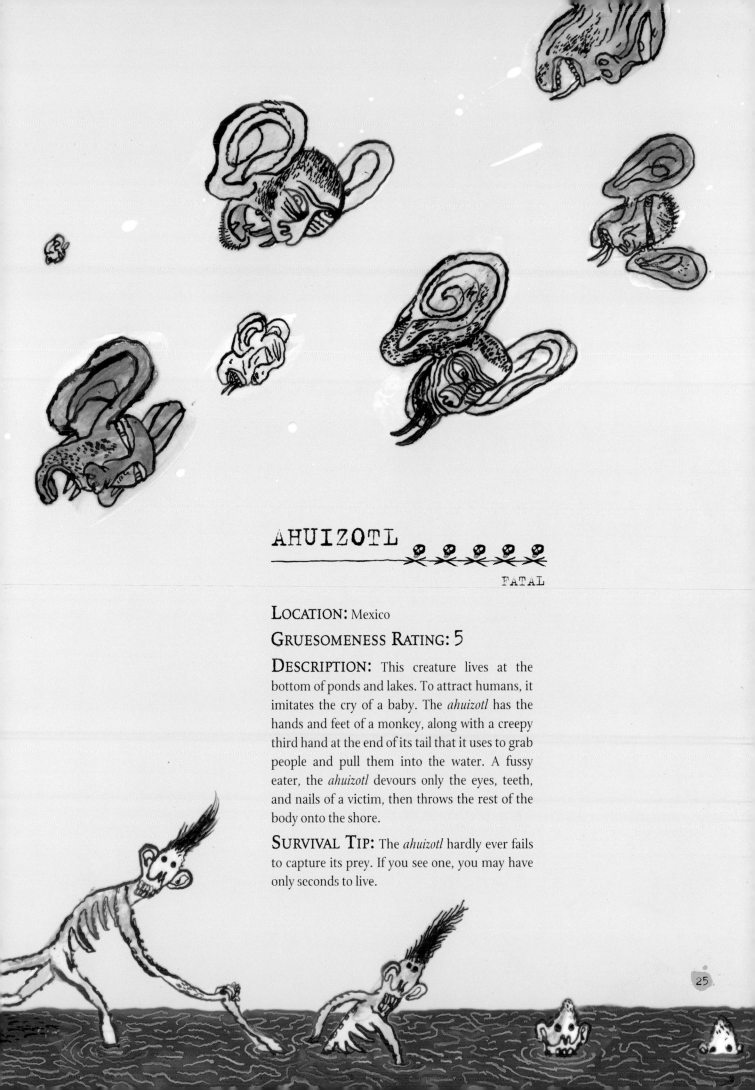

AHUIZOTL

FATAL

LOCATION: Mexico

GRUESOMENESS RATING: 5

DESCRIPTION: This creature lives at the bottom of ponds and lakes. To attract humans, it imitates the cry of a baby. The *ahuizotl* has the hands and feet of a monkey, along with a creepy third hand at the end of its tail that it uses to grab people and pull them into the water. A fussy eater, the *ahuizotl* devours only the eyes, teeth, and nails of a victim, then throws the rest of the body onto the shore.

SURVIVAL TIP: The *ahuizotl* hardly ever fails to capture its prey. If you see one, you may have only seconds to live.

HUECÚ

VERY DANGEROUS

LOCATION: Chile

GRUESOMENESS RATING: 3

DESCRIPTION: Deep in Andean mountain lakes live enormous squid-like creatures called *huecú*. When a *huecú* comes to the surface, it looks like a cow's hide spread out on the water, except that hundreds of eyeballs rim the outer edge. On top of the body are four bigger eyes. The *huecú* grabs unsuspecting people and animals with its tentacles, pulls them into the water, and eats them.

SURVIVAL TIP: To injure a *huecú* and give yourself time to escape, throw branches of the spiny *quisco* bush at it.

TAQUATÚ

USUALLY FATAL

LOCATION: Tierra del Fuego

GRUESOMENESS RATING: 4

DESCRIPTION: This invisible cannibal giant travels in an equally invisible canoe that can sail on water and through the air. The *taquatú* seizes unsuspecting travelers and carries them off to cook and eat.

SURVIVAL TIP: The wake of the *taquatú*'s canoe is visible as it plows through the water, and tree branches bend as it glides through the air. If you watch carefully for these signs, you may have time to escape.

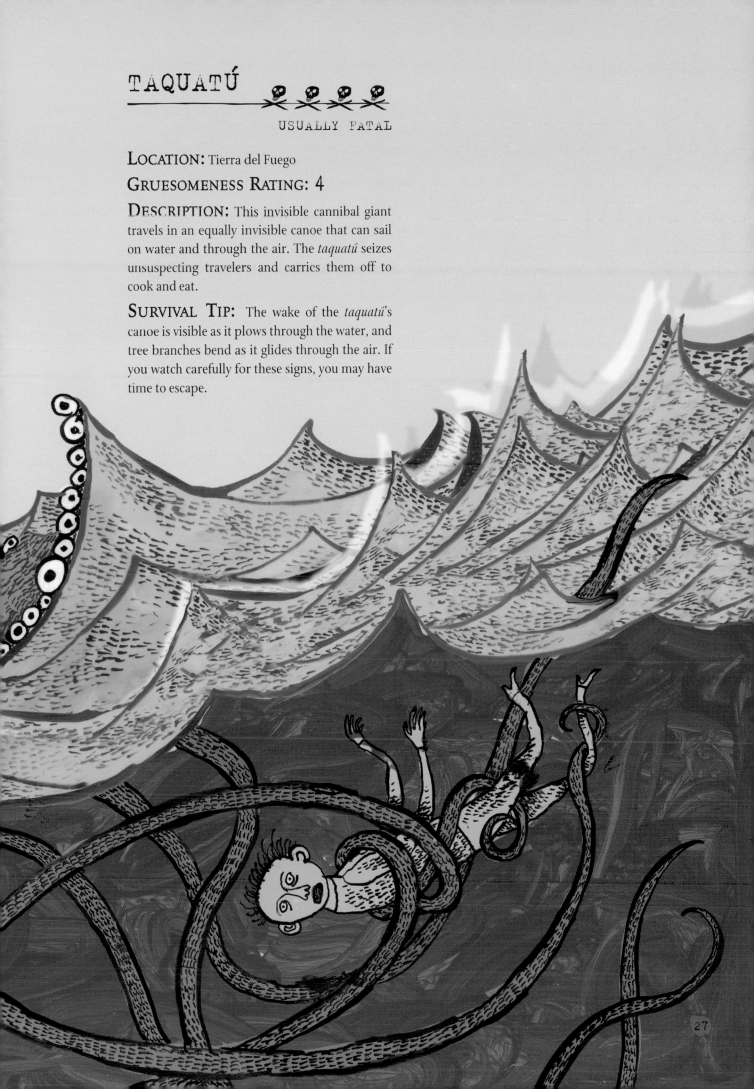

NÄKK

LOCATION: Sweden

GRUESOMENESS RATING: 3

DESCRIPTION: A *näkk* is a shape-changer who lives in deep and dangerous waters, especially in whirlpools. Each *näkk* must claim a human victim every year. He may take the shape of something irresistible, such as a jeweled necklace or a beautiful horse. When someone goes near the water to seize this unexpected treasure, the *näkk* grabs him. Or a *näkk* may change into a handsome man and go to a dance, where he hypnotizes a woman and waltzes her into the water.

SURVIVAL TIP: You can escape a *näkk* by speaking his name aloud or by saying, "*Nyk, nyk,* needle in the water, you sink, I float."

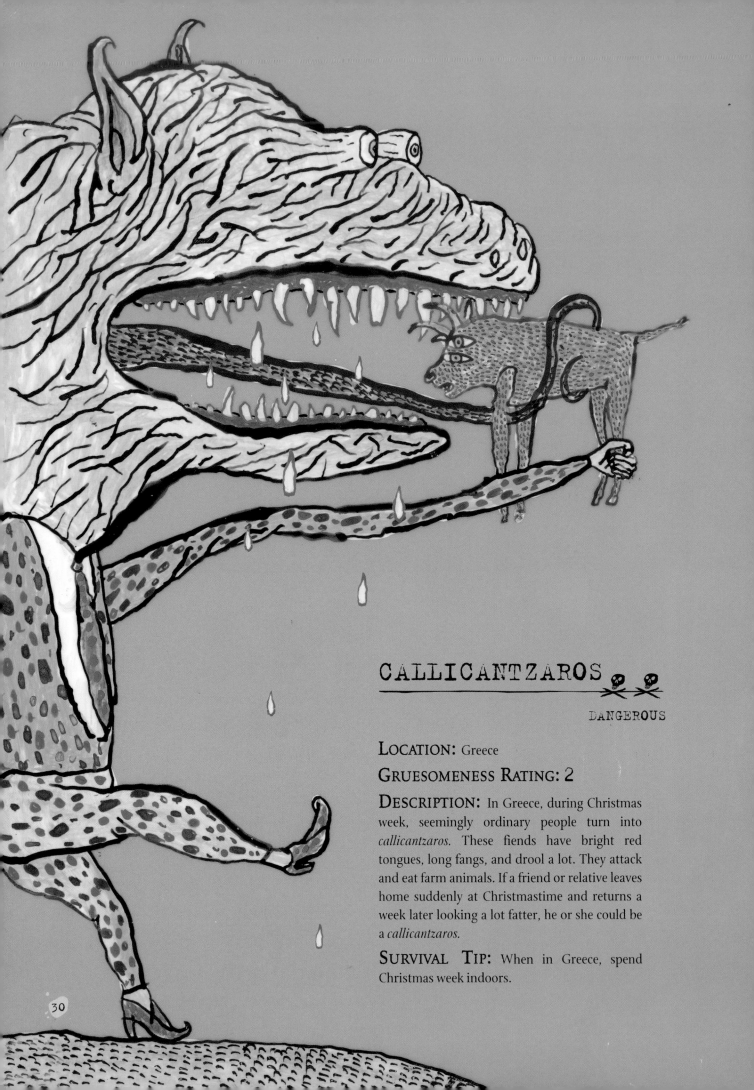

CALLICANTZAROS ☠ ☠

DANGEROUS

LOCATION: Greece

GRUESOMENESS RATING: 2

DESCRIPTION: In Greece, during Christmas week, seemingly ordinary people turn into *callicantzaros*. These fiends have bright red tongues, long fangs, and drool a lot. They attack and eat farm animals. If a friend or relative leaves home suddenly at Christmastime and returns a week later looking a lot fatter, he or she could be a *callicantzaros*.

SURVIVAL TIP: When in Greece, spend Christmas week indoors.

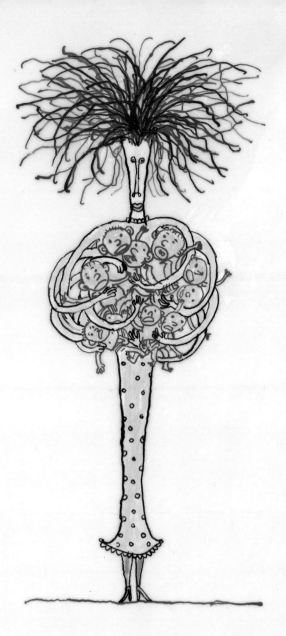

DZIWOZONY

DANGEROUS

LOCATION: Poland

GRUESOMENESS RATING: 2

DESCRIPTION: The *dziwozony* are wild women who dwell in caves deep in the forest. They are extremely tall and thin, have tangled hair, long fingers, and tiny feet. They watch for children who stray into the forest, and take them to their caves. They absolutely adore children and feed them well, but because the *dziwozony* do not know their own strength, they are likely to tickle them to death or smother them with kisses.

SURVIVAL TIP: If you are small and cute, don't venture alone into a Polish forest.

OVDA

DANGEROUS

LOCATION: Finland

GRUESOMENESS RATING: 2

DESCRIPTION: Travelers often hear *ovda* laughing and clapping their hands in the forest. *Ovda* love to play mean tricks and joke about them afterward. One of their favorite pranks is to approach a man, challenge him to a wrestling match, then tickle him to death.

SURVIVAL TIP: An *ovda* will become powerless if you touch its left armpit.

31

NOCNITSA

DANGEROUS

LOCATION: Bulgaria

GRUESOMENESS RATING: 2

DESCRIPTION: When young children cry at night and cannot sleep, these invisible demons may be pinching them, tickling them, or even sucking their blood.

SURVIVAL TIP: With a knife, draw a circle on the floor around the child's bed. If the *nocnitsa* still bothers the child, bury a doll, an ax, and a spindle under the floor beneath the bed.

VUKODLAK

LOCATION: Serbia

GRUESOMENESS RATING: 4

DESCRIPTION: A *vukodlak* is a wicked person—a murderer, for instance—who lives on after death. He arises from his grave and sneaks about at night, sucking the life force from his relatives, beginning with the youngest, then from everyone else in the neighborhood. A *vukodlak* looks like a person whose skin has been blown up like a balloon.

SURVIVAL TIP: A good spirit called a *kresnik* can protect a house from *vukodlak*s. It is not possible to buy or hire a *kresnik*, however. Either they live in a house or they don't. They especially like houses that the same family has owned for many generations. A wooden stake through the heart will also stop a *vukodlak*.

ANKOU

FATAL

LOCATION: France

GRUESOMENESS RATING: 5

DESCRIPTION: The *ankou*, a living skeleton, drives the death cart that arrives at a house just before someone dies. As the *ankou* whips the horse that pulls the cart, his head revolves around and around on his neck. Only the person who is about to die sees the *ankou* and his cart or hears his knock at the door.

SURVIVAL TIP: Not applicable.

SPUNKIE

DANGEROUS

LOCATION: Scotland

GRUESOMENESS RATING: 2

DESCRIPTION: This tiny glowing creature appears to people who are walking alone at night. It looks just like the light of a house, but it is mischievous, shifting, alive, and evil. Spunkies enjoy leading people off cliffs in the darkness.

SURVIVAL TIP: Beware of anything glowing in the gloaming.

METS-HALDIJAS

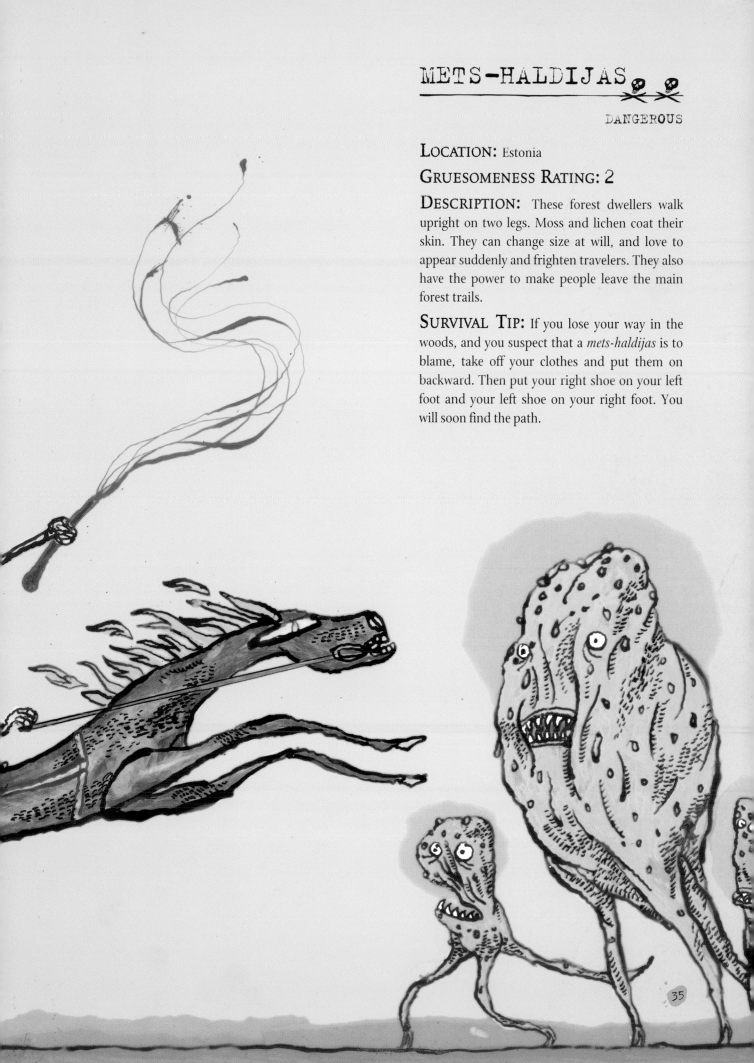

DANGEROUS

LOCATION: Estonia

GRUESOMENESS RATING: 2

DESCRIPTION: These forest dwellers walk upright on two legs. Moss and lichen coat their skin. They can change size at will, and love to appear suddenly and frighten travelers. They also have the power to make people leave the main forest trails.

SURVIVAL TIP: If you lose your way in the woods, and you suspect that a *mets-haldijas* is to blame, take off your clothes and put them on backward. Then put your right shoe on your left foot and your left shoe on your right foot. You will soon find the path.

PRICOLICI

LOCATION: Romania

GRUESOMENESS RATING: 4

DESCRIPTION: *Pricolici* are the seventh son or seventh daughter in a family, and are born with short tails. They can transform into werewolves by turning nine somersaults in a row, and they roam about (usually on the night before a holiday) attacking anyone who is traveling alone.

SURVIVAL TIP: *Pricolici* hate the smell and taste of garlic. On the night before any Romanian holiday (check the local calendar), sew garlic into your clothes, string garlic cloves into necklaces and bracelets, and rub garlic juice on all doors and windows.

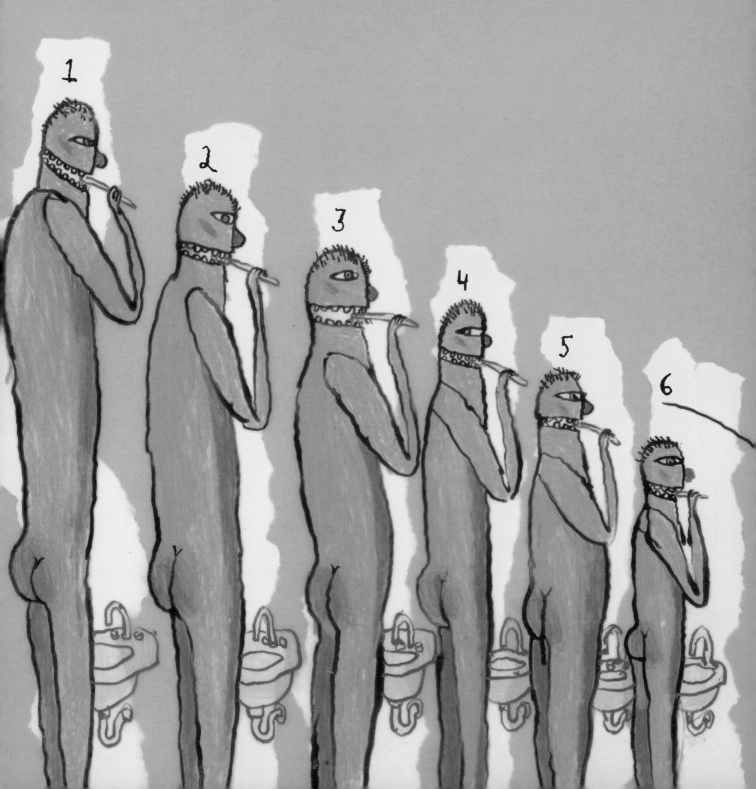

MORA

DANGEROUS

LOCATION: Russia

GRUESOMENESS RATING: 2

DESCRIPTION: Rather than eat people or scare them to death, a *mora* prefers to slowly drive them crazy. These invisible creatures live in houses and torment the inhabitants by messing up their work—tangling the threads of their embroidery, for example, or burning their stews and sauces. They also enjoy creating bad dreams.

SURVIVAL TIP: If you suspect that a *mora* is bothering you, sleep with a mirror and a broom next to your bed, and it will leave the house.

7

GRYLA

VERY DANGEROUS

LOCATION: Iceland

GRUESOMENESS RATING: 3

DESCRIPTION: *Gryla* is a particularly nasty troll. She has a dozen heads, each with three eyes. *Gryla*'s few teeth are long and pointy. She constantly twists and turns each head on its neck, so that she can see in every direction. She is looking for children to put in her sack, take home, toast, and eat.

SURVIVAL TIP: Like many other child-stealing monsters, *Gryla* shows a distinct preference for ill-behaved youngsters.

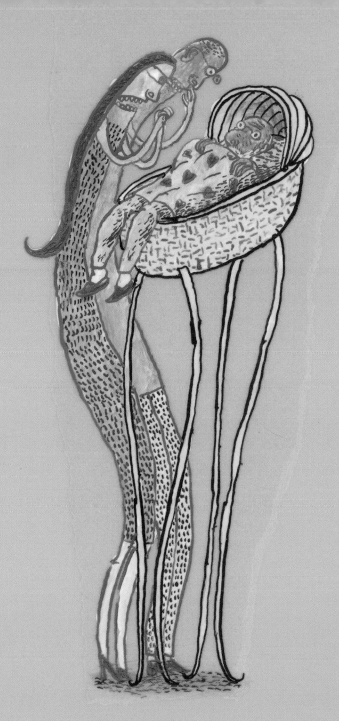

GOOD PEOPLE AND CHANGELINGS ☠ ☠

DANGEROUS

LOCATION: Ireland

GRUESOMENESS RATING: 2

DESCRIPTION: People call these beings "good" in the hope that they may act that way, but they seldom do. The good people live under the earth and beneath lakes, and they enter the daylight world in order to steal human babies and leave their own unwanted old people in their place. If a healthy baby suddenly looks shriveled and old, he is probably one of these changelings.

SURVIVAL TIP: A changeling must leave if anyone makes him laugh. If you suspect that a baby is a changeling, try doing something completely ridiculous. The changeling will laugh and run away. Soon the good people will return the real baby.

POLUDNITSA ☠ ☠ ☠

VERY DANGEROUS

LOCATION: Russia

GRUESOMENESS RATING: 3

DESCRIPTION: The *poludnitsa* is a shimmering spirit that appears in the grain fields at midday. She asks difficult riddles, and if you cannot tell her the correct answers, you will probably not be seen alive again.

SURVIVAL TIP: Take riddle books with you to Russia and study them every day.

JINN

LOCATION: North and Central Africa

GRUESOMENESS RATING: 5

DESCRIPTION: Jinn are huge, horrible creatures. Their faces and bodies are somewhat human, but they have wings on their backs, hooves on their feet, and horns on their heads. They kidnap people and cause diseases. The child of a human and a jinn looks human but has the ability to walk through walls and fly, and never seems to grow old.

SURVIVAL TIP: You're on your own.

GHUL

USUALLY FATAL

LOCATION: North Africa

GRUESOMENESS RATING: 4

DESCRIPTION: A *ghul* can take many forms. One of its favorite shapes is a creature with wings and legs like an ostrich, a long snout and sharp teeth, and one eye. *Ghul* live in uninhabited places, and they capture men travelers by changing into pretty young women who call out to them. When the men approach, the *ghul* devour them.

SURVIVAL TIP: Memorize the meaning of *uninhabited*.

ABIKU

LOCATION: Nigeria, Benin, and Togo

GRUESOMENESS RATING: 2

DESCRIPTION: The invisible *abiku* are always ravenously hungry and thirsty. An *abiku* will secretly enter the body of a child and steal the food the parents feed her, then share the food with its *abiku* friends who lurk nearby. A child whose hunger is never satisfied may be the victim of an *abiku*.

SURVIVAL TIP: To rid a child of an *abiku*, hang a bell around her neck. *Abiku* cannot stand the sound of bells.

WOKOLO

LOCATION: Mali

GRUESOMENESS RATING: 2

DESCRIPTION: Even though they are no taller than a five-year-old child, the *wokolo* are stronger than the strongest man. *Wokolo* come out only at night. They can see through walls, and when they spy something they want, they become invisible, enter the house, and take it. They also kidnap children.

SURVIVAL TIP: Children should wear special anti-*wokolo* hats (available at local shops).

CHIRUWI

USUALLY FATAL

LOCATION: Malawi

GRUESOMENESS RATING: 4

DESCRIPTION: The *chiruwi* is a giant half-bird with one wing, one leg, and one eye. If a *chiruwi* challenges you to wrestle, you cannot refuse, and if you lose the wrestling match, you will die. If you win, however, the *chiruwi* will show you the secrets of plants so that you can become a doctor.

SURVIVAL TIP: Work out regularly.

NDILE

USUALLY FATAL

LOCATION: Sierra Leone

GRUESOMENESS RATING: 4

DESCRIPTION: The *ndile* is a vampire snake created by a sorcerer. The sorcerer steals a piece of clothing from his intended victim, then buries it close to that person's home. At night, the clothing turns into a snake and sucks the person's blood. If you awaken in the morning feeling weak and tired, you could be the victim of a *ndile*.

SURVIVAL TIP: To end the attacks, you must find and destroy the buried cloth. Be careful, though. This cloth is so powerful that touching it can give you a fatal electric shock.

KISHI

LOCATION: Zimbabwe

GRUESOMENESS RATING: 4

DESCRIPTION: A *kishi* has two faces. His human face is quite handsome. His other face, which is on the back of his head, is that of a hyena and has huge, sharp teeth. With his hyena face, the *kishi* attacks and eats people.

SURVIVAL TIP: Observe strangers carefully. In order to hide his hyena face, a *kishi* wears his hair puffed up and twisted into braids.

NKANYAMBA ☠ ☠ ☠ ☠

USUALLY FATAL

LOCATION: South Africa

GRUESOMENESS RATING: 4

DESCRIPTION: The *nkanyamba* is a serpent that dwells in deep pools. She emerges from the water whirling like a tornado and kidnaps people. Once, a *nkanyamba* took a man to live with her underwater as her husband. Later, the man escaped. He had turned completely white, and his hair was long, straight, and seaweed green. He could no longer speak and would eat only live frogs, crabs, and lizards.

SURVIVAL TIP: Avoiding the *nkanyamba*'s habitat is your best hope.

NUNDU

LOCATION: Southern and Eastern Africa

GRUESOMENESS RATING: 5

DESCRIPTION: This monster takes the shape of a lion or leopard—terrifying enough—but when it approaches a human, the *nundu* opens its mouth wider and wider until it is as large as a cave. Then the monster inhales, swallowing its victim in one bite.

SURVIVAL TIP: Good luck!

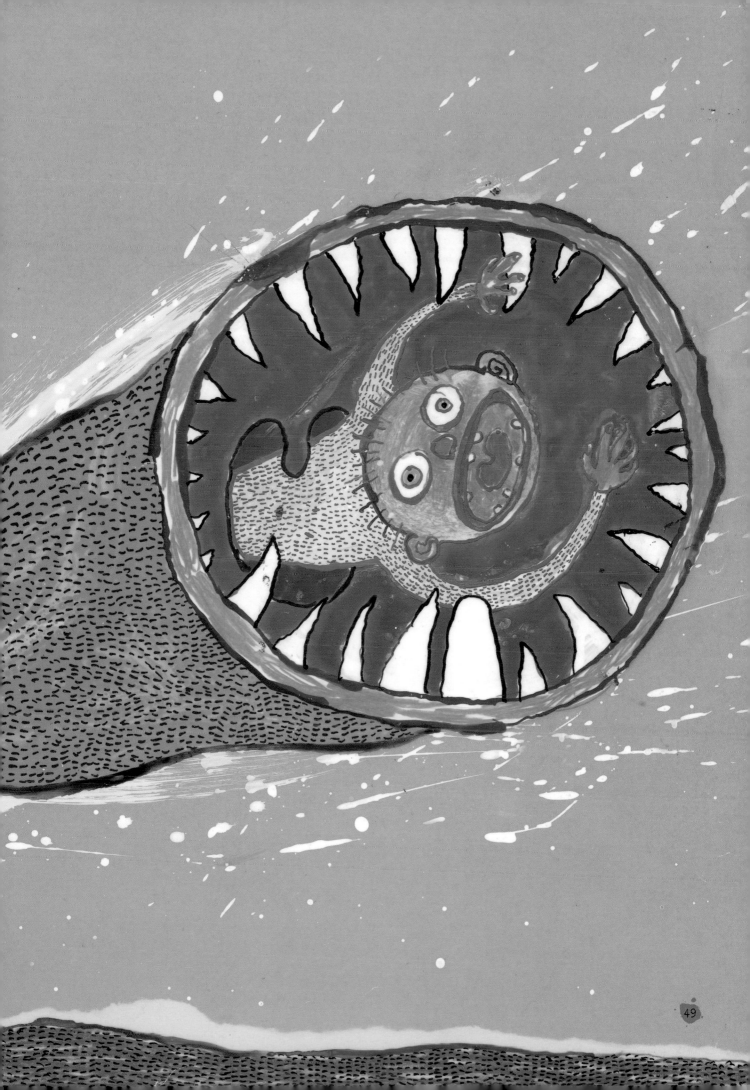

Asia and the Pacific

RAKSASA

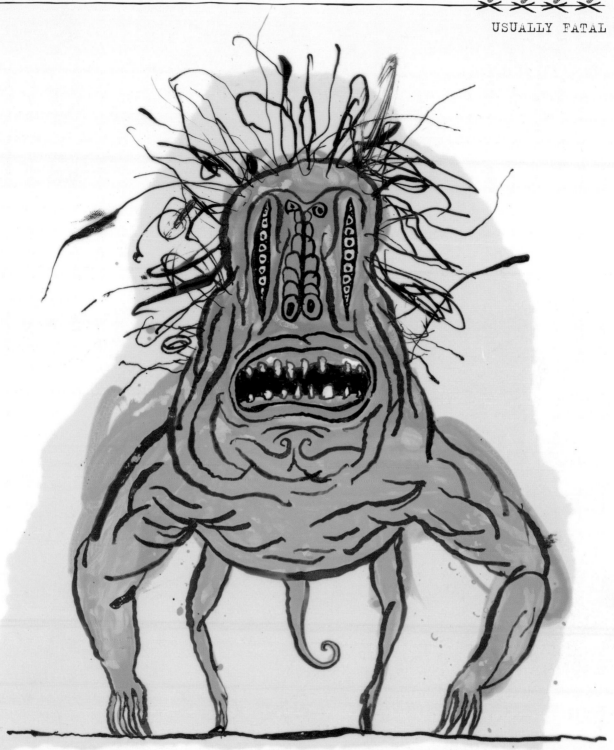

LOCATION: India

GRUESOMENESS RATING: 4

DESCRIPTION: *Raksasas'* faces are either green or blue, and they have tusky yellow teeth and matted hair. Their eyes are vertical slits. *Raksasas* can make themselves look like ordinary people when they want to, but they can't disguise the fact that their fingers are attached backward to their hands. They like to capture and eat children.

SURVIVAL TIP: Call the *raksasa* "cousin" or "uncle." It is taboo for a *raksasa* to eat anyone who is related to him.

BAKU

Bad dream

LOCATION: Japan

GRUESOMENESS RATING: 1

DESCRIPTION: After reading about so many evil creatures, you will probably want to know about this helpful one. The *baku* has a hairy head, a long trunk, and two tusks, like an elephant. Its skin is spotted, and it has the tail of an ox. It comes into your bedroom at night and eats your bad dreams. To summon the *baku*, just before bedtime say, *"Baku kurae."*

POLONG and PELESIT

DANGEROUS

LOCATION: Malaysia

GRUESOMENESS RATING: 2

DESCRIPTION: A *polong* is about the size of a fingertip and looks like a little person. The *pelesit* resembles a cricket. Both of them live in a bottle and do the bidding of a *jinjangan* sorcerer. The *polong* and *pelesit* fly off together at their master's bidding to make someone sick. First, the *pelesit* drills a hole in the person's skin with its sharp tail and enters the body. The *polong* follows after. People with *polong* sickness talk endlessly about cats.

SURVIVAL TIP: Ask the sick person, "Who is your master?" He will answer in a high-pitched voice (the voice of the *polong*) and reveal the name of the sorcerer. He will be cured immediately.

KUMO

LOCATION: Japan

GRUESOMENESS RATING: 3

DESCRIPTION: Kumo, the giant spider, has eyes as big as saucers, legs as long as a horse's, and very sharp teeth. It hides in houses, where it collapses in a corner, looking exactly like a futon. If a person sits down on the fake futon, she quickly becomes entangled in the kumo's sticky web and ends up spider dinner.

SURVIVAL TIP: Look under futons for long, hairy legs.

KAPPA

DANGEROUS

LOCATION: Japan

GRUESOMENESS RATING: 2

DESCRIPTION: *Kappa* are small hairy creatures about as tall as a three-year-old child, with the head of a monkey and the body of a tortoise. They hide in rivers and streams, where they bite people and suck their blood.

SURVIVAL TIP: *Kappa* adore cucumbers. For protection against *kappa* attacks, carve your name and birth date into a cucumber and throw it in the water. The *kappa* will eat the cucumber and leave you alone.

MANSUSOPSOP

DANGEROUS

LOCATION: Philippines

GRUESOMENESS RATING: 2

DESCRIPTION: This huge bat has a long thin tongue with a sharp point at the end. It hovers above houses at night, lowers its tongue through the roof, and sucks the blood of the people sleeping inside.

SURVIVAL TIP: Don't sleep in houses with grass roofs.

XIANG SHI

USUALLY FATAL

LOCATION: China

GRUESOMENESS RATING: 4

DESCRIPTION: Sometimes a corpse does not decay but rises from the grave at night, sneaks into houses, and sucks the blood of the living. The *xiang shi* has green skin, red eyes, and long twisted fingernails. Whitish fur grows on its body.

SURVIVAL TIP: The *xiang shi* can never touch water, so you can escape its clutches by swimming a river or a stream. The creature can be completely destroyed only if its body is dug up during the day and burned.

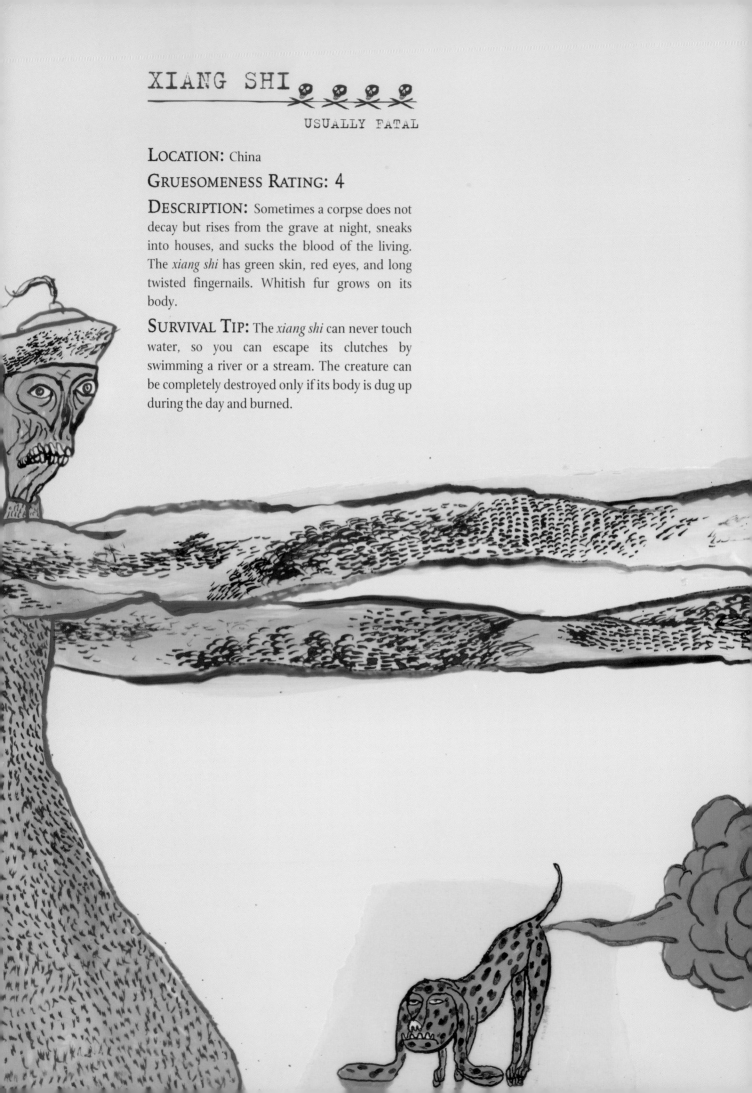

KILIAKAI

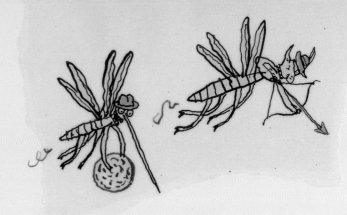

LOCATION: New Guinea

GRUESOMENESS RATING: 2

DESCRIPTION: These creatures live near streams and shoot arrows that cause malaria. The *kiliakai* carry magic *pipu* stones, which cure any disease. Sometimes they drop these stones and lucky people find them.

SURVIVAL TIP: Seek *pipu* stones at your own risk.

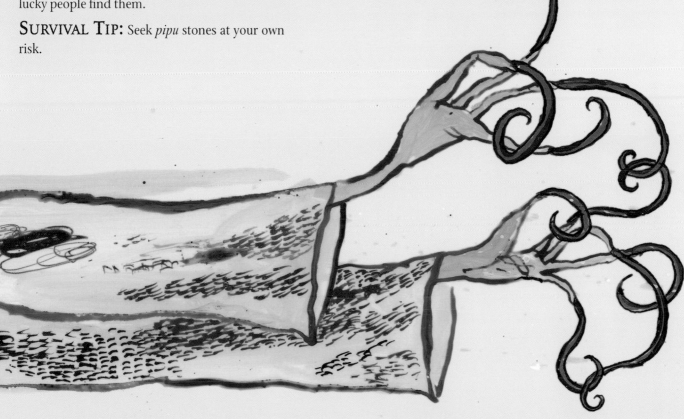

SIGBIN

VERY DANGEROUS

LOCATION: Philippines

GRUESOMENESS RATING: 3

DESCRIPTION: A *sigbin* is about the size and shape of a beagle, but its hind end is higher than its front end, and its long ears drag on the ground. It can fly, using its ears as wings. The intestinal gas of the *sigbin* is fatal.

SURVIVAL TIP: Never walk or stand downwind of a *sigbin*. If you learn the proper magic spells, you will be able to tame this creature and ride it through the air.

MARAKI-HAU

LOCATION: New Zealand

GRUESOMENESS RATING: 5

DESCRIPTION: This sea creature has the body of a snake, an enormous human head, and the tail of a fish. It uses its hollow tongue like a vacuum cleaner hose, sucking up fishing parties, boats and all.

SURVIVAL TIP: None available.

BUNYIP

LOCATION: Australia

GRUESOMENESS RATING: 4

DESCRIPTION: This creature has a flat face and a fish tail and looks like a cross between a seal and a hippopotamus. *Bunyips* live in water holes, and in the dry season they burrow into the mud and wait for their victims.

SURVIVAL TIP: The *bunyip* emits a low, unearthly howl. Run the other way when you hear it.

BHUTA

DANGEROUS

LOCATION: India

GRUESOMENESS RATING: 2

DESCRIPTION: *Bhuta* are short, have red faces, wear their hair in braids, and speak in high, nasal voices. If you should meet one, it might seem to be human, but you will notice that it casts no shadow. They live inside trees, in old wells, and in deserted houses.

SURVIVAL TIP: When local people suspect that a certain place is the home of a *bhuta*, they pile rocks nearby to warn others away, so be on the lookout for these. If you think you see a *bhuta*, lie flat on the ground. The creature is unable to look downward and will not see you.

DOGAI

LOCATION: Vanuatu

GRUESOMENESS RATING: 2

DESCRIPTION: *Dogai* look like normal women, except that their tattoos are far more beautiful and their hair is bleached to a lighter shade of blonde. Their knee and elbow joints are reversed, and sometimes their heads are backward as well. If a man marries a *dogai,* she will eat him.

SURVIVAL TIP: Before befriending a woman in Vanuatu, go for a walk together and notice which way her knees bend.

LEGASELEP

LOCATION: Caroline Islands

GRUESOMENESS RATING: 3

DESCRIPTION: *Legaseleps* are giants with ten to twelve heads. They travel from island to island in enormous canoes, looking for human beings to eat. *Legaseleps* are afraid of loud noises and fairly stupid.

SURVIVAL TIP: A girl once killed a *legaselep* by placing a barnacle under her tongue before the *legaselep* swallowed her. Then she used the sharp shell of the barnacle to cut her way out of the monster's stomach.

ADARO

VERY DANGEROUS

LOCATION: Solomon Islands

GRUESOMENESS RATING: 3

DESCRIPTION: The *adaro* lives in the ocean and is often seen sliding along the rainbow. He looks like a man, but has a fish tail on each heel and a shark's fin on top of his head. For no apparent reason, the *adaro* throws poisonous flying fish at people.

SURVIVAL TIP: Be prepared to dodge flying objects.

TAUA

LOCATION: New Britain

GRUESOMENESS RATING: 5

DESCRIPTION: This fish can go on living even after it is cooked, chewed, and swallowed. If you should have the bad luck to eat a *taua* fish for dinner, you will hear it laughing inside your stomach just before it begins to digest you.

SURVIVAL TIP: Identify all fish before you eat them—otherwise it will be too late.

AFTERWORD

Every one of the world's cultures has its own monsters, and in the prescientific era most people believed in these monsters at least some of the time. Stories about them often play a necessary role in people's lives. For example, adults tell children about the creatures that dwell in treacherous waters and in caves, forests, and abandoned buildings. These stories prevent all but the most foolish child from wandering into dangerous terrain. Other tales warn adults against falling for the charms of attractive strangers of the opposite sex. Some monsters in this book embody widespread beliefs about forest spirits who protect animals and punish hunters who take too much game. These beliefs help preserve the balance of nature. When tales are told about people who fall victim to monsters, more often than not these individuals, either foolishly or intentionally, violated the rules of their culture.

Some monsters possess special healing powers or healing objects, which crafty humans can acquire. The most repulsive monsters in world traditions were used to explain sickness, especially contagious diseases. Before scientists discovered bacteria and viruses, people invented tales of invisible and night-traveling ghouls who made people sicken and die. Indeed, they were correct that the cause of most diseases is invisible. A sad result of these beliefs, though, was that sometimes innocent people in the community were accused of being shape-changers or sorcerers who intentionally spread illness. These scapegoats were often persecuted or even put to death.

The nature and behavior of monsters are closely related to the fears and desires of the people who invented them. Consider the monsters in this book, and imagine what needs each creature fulfilled. Did they explain strange or unpleasant events? Did they remind people to be especially cautious? Or were they embodiments of frightening aspects of nature? When you travel, you can collect your own monster tales by asking people about local unfriendly creatures, spirits, and haunted places.

Text copyright © 2005 by Judy Sierra. Illustrations copyright © 2005 by Henrik Drescher. All rights reserved. First edition 2005. Library of Congress Cataloging-in-Publication Data is available. Library of Congress Catalog Card Number 2004057470. ISBN 0-7636-1727-X. Printed in Singapore. This book was typeset in Stone Print and Trixie Text. The illustrations were done in mixed media. Candlewick Press, 2067 Massachusetts Avenue, Cambridge, Massachusetts 02140. Visit us at www.candlewick.com. 10 9 8 7 6 5 4 3